# YOU CHOOSE
BOOKS

# WAR IN AFGHANISTAN

## AN INTERACTIVE MODERN HISTORY ADVENTURE

by Matt Doeden and Blake Hoena

Consultant:
Michael Doidge
Military Historian

**CAPSTONE PRESS**
a capstone imprint

You Choose Books are published by Capstone Press,
1710 Roe Crest Drive, North Mankato, Minnesota 56003
www.capstonepub.com

**Library of Congress Cataloging-in-Publication Data**
Doeden, Matt.
War in Afghanistan: an interactive modern history adventure / by Matt Doeden
and Blake Hoena.
pages cm.—(You choose. You choose: modern)
Includes bibliographical references and index.
Summary: "Describes the people and events of the U.S. war in Afghanistan. The reader's
choices reveal the historical details"—Provided by publisher.
Audience: Grades 4-6.
ISBN 978-1-4765-4190-7 (library binding)
ISBN 978-1-4765-5221-7 (paperback)
ISBN 978-1-4765-6067-0 (ebook PDF)
1. Afghan War, 2001—Juvenile literature. 2. Combat—Juvenile literature. 3. Tactics—
Juvenile literature. 4. Military convoys—United States—Juvenile literature. 5. Special
forces (Military science)—United States—Juvenile literature. I. Hoena, B. A. II. Title.
DS371.412.D53 2014
958.104'7—dc23                     2013036664

**Editorial Credits**
Catherine Neitge and Angie Kaelberer, editors; Gene Bentdahl, designer;
Wanda Winch, media researcher; Jennifer Walker, production specialist

**Photo Credits**
AP Images: Brennan Linsley, 73, 91; Capstone, 10; Getty Images Inc., 19, Getty
Images Inc: AFP/David Furst, cover, Joe Raedle, 12, 16, 25, 102, MCT/*Fort Worth
Star-Telegram*/Tom Pennington, 28, U.S. Army photo, 37; Shutterstock: Francisco
Caravana, soil background, Lexy Sinnot, 42; U.S. Air Force: Tech Sgt. Efron Lopez, 81,
96; U.S. Army: 2nd Lt. Jeff Hall, 6, Cpl. James Clark, 70, Sgt. Justin Howe, 59, Sgt. Ken
Scar, 7th MPAD, 38, 41, 44, 52, 63, 67, Spc. Daniel P. Schook, 47, Spc. Daniel Petty,
77, Spc. David Marck Jr., 14, 34, 105, Staff Sgt. Robert Hyatt, 8; U.S. Marine Corps:
Col. Andrew Carlson, 99, Cpl. Jeff Drew, 85

Printed in the United States of America in Stevens Point, Wisconsin.
092013         007765WZS14

# TABLE OF CONTENTS

# ABOUT YOUR ADVENTURE

YOU are fighting in the longest war in U.S. history—the war in Afghanistan.

In this book you'll explore how the choices people made meant the difference between life and death. The events you'll experience happened to real people.

Chapter One sets the scene. Then you choose which path to read. Follow the directions at the bottom of each page. The choices you make will change your outcome. After you finish your path, go back and read the others for new perspectives and more adventures.

*YOU CHOOSE the path*
*you take through history.*

U.S. Army and Afghan soldiers investigate a roadside attack in eastern Afghanistan.

# A Long War

The war in Afghanistan is the longest war in U.S. history. American troops and their allies have been fighting there since 2001. The fighting began soon after the terrorist group al-Qaeda hijacked airplanes to attack New York City and Washington, D.C., on September 11, 2001.

Afghanistan is located in South Asia. The Taliban governed the country from 1996 until 2001. The Taliban is an Islamic group that has ties to terrorist groups, including al-Qaeda.

7

After the 2001 attacks, U.S. officials demanded that the Taliban turn over al-Qaeda leader Osama bin Laden. Bin Laden had gone into hiding in Afghanistan.

Turn the page.

Canadian soldiers joined the search for Taliban fighters in 2002.

When the Taliban refused, the United States began military strikes in Afghanistan. The first goal of the war was to remove the Taliban from power. Achieving that goal didn't take long.

The United States used its military forces to drive the Taliban out of Afghanistan's major cities. The North Atlantic Treaty Organization (NATO) also sent soldiers from other countries to help the U.S. troops. The Taliban went into hiding, but the war was far from over.

The United States and an Afghan group, the Northern Alliance, set up a new government. It was called the Islamic Republic of Afghanistan. The new goal became protecting that government and defeating the remaining Taliban resistance.

Turn the page.

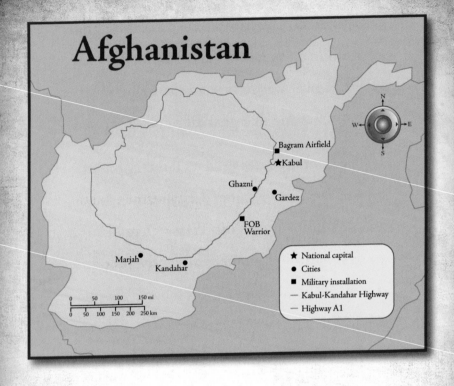

Afghanistan

- ★ National capital
- ● Cities
- ■ Military installation
- — Kabul-Kandahar Highway
- — Highway A1

Bagram Airfield
★Kabul
Ghazni
Gardez
FOB Warrior
Marjah
Kandahar

0  50  100  150 mi
0  50  100  150  200  250 km

Meanwhile, U.S. forces searched for al-Qaeda members in Afghanistan and nearby Pakistan. They captured and killed several key al-Qaeda leaders. The search for bin Laden took almost 10 years. U.S. Navy SEALs killed him in Pakistan in 2011.

The war continued after bin Laden's death. Stabilizing the Afghan government has been difficult. Taliban fighters have continued their attacks. U.S. officials fear what might happen if U.S. forces leave.

What if you could step back in time to key moments in the war? What choices would you make? How would they affect the people around you?

To join an Army Ranger rescue team during Operation Anaconda, turn to page **13**.

To protect a convoy carrying supplies for U.S. troops, turn to page **39**.

To serve as a Marine during Operation Moshtarak, turn to page **71**.

British Royal Air Force Chinook helicopters return from a mission during Operation Anaconda.

# CHAPTER 2

# Operation Anaconda

Sand whips through the air as two MH-47E Chinook helicopters prepare to lift off from Bagram Airfield in eastern Afghanistan. The whir of the helicopter blades almost drowns out the voice of your commanding officer, Army Ranger Captain Tim Reynolds. You're nervous and excited. It's early in March 2002, and this is the first action you'll be seeing in the two months you've been deployed to Afghanistan.

The U.S. military and its allies have been successful so far. The Taliban has been driven from power. But their forces are gathered with al-Qaeda fighters in the Arma Mountains of eastern Afghanistan. They are using a mountain valley as a training site and staging area to launch attacks.

Turn the page.

U.S. soldiers scan the area for enemy fighters during Operation Anaconda.

Just three days ago, U.S. forces launched Operation Anaconda. The operation's goal is to use the mountains to observe the enemy training site, and if needed, order airstrikes on enemy activity. Earlier today a team of Navy SEALs tried to take control of a mountain, but they met too much resistance. Some SEALs are trapped on the mountain.

"The Chinook carrying the SEAL team went down," Reynolds yells. "The SEALs are under heavy fire and need our help. Let's go."

Reynolds climbs aboard a helicopter, called Mustang 1, which will lead the way. The other helicopter, Mustang 2, will follow. Mustang 1 is more likely to see action, but Mustang 2 could be safer.

To board Mustang 1 with Captain Reynolds, turn to page **16**.

To take command of Mustang 2, turn to page **19**.

An Army gunner is at the ready in the door of a Chinook helicopter.

Mustang 1 speeds toward the mountain. You hear Reynolds and the pilot, Lieutenant Jeff Baker, talking on the radio. There seems to be some confusion about where you're supposed to land, but you know that isn't your concern. Your eyes are on the rocky ground below.

The mountain's snow-capped peak stands at more than 10,000 feet. The peak is rough, and the enemy is already dug in for a fight. Baker is bringing the Chinook down when you hear gunfire. The enemy is attacking! Bullets pelt the chopper. You hear someone shout in pain. One of the helicopter's gunners has been shot. Before you can react, an explosion rocks the helicopter. It's a rocket-propelled grenade (RPG)! The helicopter lurches and then crashes onto the rocky mountain below.

The enemy continues to fire. Bullets rip through the cockpit's glass. Several more of your men are hit.

"Everyone out!" Reynolds shouts. He yells to you, "Lieutenant, get your squad behind cover and return fire!"

Turn the page.

Smoke hangs in the air as you rush out of the helicopter, making it hard to see where to go. Corporal Brandon Doss crumples to the ground, struck by an enemy bullet. He needs help, but will you be shot if you go to his aid?

To head for cover behind nearby boulders, turn to page **24**.

To help Corporal Doss, turn to page **30**.

An Army gunner scans the Afghan mountains from a helicopter.

You look out the cockpit window as Mustang 2 lifts off and speeds toward the mountain. The ground below you is rough. It's cold and rocky, with patches of snow at the highest points.

Turn the page.

As you approach your landing zone, Mustang 2 circles as Mustang 1 goes in. You hear gunshots. Boom! An explosion rocks Mustang 1's right side, severely damaging one of its engines. The helicopter goes into a tailspin and crashes to the ground. The pilot quickly brings Mustang 2 up to a safer distance.

"Should we go down and help them?" asks the pilot, Lieutenant Jason Harbo.

Your first instinct is to say yes. Your fellow Rangers are in trouble. But landing here would put you within range of the enemy fighters who fired on Mustang 1. Maybe it's better to find somewhere else to land.

To order the pilot to find another landing zone, go to page **21.**

To order him to descend and help the Mustang 1 team, turn to page **31**

We can't land here," you tell Harbo. "Pull back."

You feel terrible about leaving your fellow Rangers behind. But landing here would be almost certain death. You discuss your options with command by radio and decide to land farther down the mountain. As you speak to your commanders, you learn that your mission has changed. The SEAL team is no longer on top of the mountain. Your mission now is to secure the mountain and capture or kill the enemy.

As the Chinook touches down, you realize how difficult your job is going to be. You have 2,000 feet of harsh, rocky, snow-covered mountain to climb. And you have to lug all your gear, weapons, and heavy body armor with you.

21

Turn the page.

"Let's go," you tell your men.

The climb is very tough. In minutes you're gasping for breath in the thin mountain air. The slope is steep and dangerous. And if that's not enough, there's the thud of enemy mortar fire coming your way. It seems only a matter of time before either the climb or the enemy kills you.

To continue the climb, go to page **23**.

To retreat down the mountain and try to find another way, turn to page **32**.

You're a Ranger, and Rangers don't quit. You hear and feel an explosion above. Some of the men cheer. They know it must be a U.S. airstrike on the enemy.

At an elevation of about 10,000 feet, the air is thin. Your lungs struggle to pull in enough oxygen. A climb that would normally take 45 minutes stretches to more than two hours. But you make it. Coming over a rise, you see the Mustang 1 team taking cover behind some boulders. Above them lies the enemy bunker, smoking from the airstrike.

Captain Reynolds greets you. "I know your men are exhausted, but the job isn't done yet. It's time to attack."

Turn to page **27**.

The rattle of enemy gunfire continues as you rush for cover behind the boulders. An explosion shakes the mountainside. A ball of flame rises from the crashed Chinook. You're glad you got out of there in time. You're relieved to see that another Ranger was able to reach Doss and drag him to safety.

The enemy is in a strong position. Their bunker is well defended. They have you outgunned. You can't afford to delay. You think you know what to do.

"Captain," you begin ....

To say, "We should set up a communications post and call in an airstrike," go to page **25.**

To say, "We should strike immediately," turn to page **34.**

A Chinook helicopter that had crash-landed was blown up by U.S. forces to keep it from falling into enemy hands.

Reynolds nods. "Yes, do it."

Within minutes you have your long-range radio gear set up and are calling the base. Your commanders have surprising news. You learn that the SEAL team you thought you were rescuing is no longer on the mountain. Now your mission is to capture or kill the enemy on the mountain.

Turn the page.

An Air Force combat controller calls for 500-pound bombs to attack the enemy bunker. You settle in and wait. Several minutes pass before you hear the sound of jets overhead. The blasts from the bombs rock the bunker. That's one problem solved.

There's even more good news. Not long after the airstrike, the Mustang 2 team walks into your site. Their chopper landed farther down the slope. They've been climbing for more than two hours. You know they're exhausted, but the time to strike is now. Reynolds gives the order, and the Mustang 2 team joins yours in the attack.

There's been no activity from the bunker since the airstrike. But you can't assume that means all is safe. Two Rangers use a heavy machine gun to lay down cover fire as you and the other Rangers charge. You run the 150 feet to the bunker as quickly as you can, but the rocky, snow-covered slope slows you down.

When you reach the bunker, you learn that the airstrikes have taken out most of the enemy fighters who were inside. You and your men use grenades and M4 rifles to take out the rest in a brief firefight. You quickly secure the bunker and set up an aid station to tend to your fellow Rangers who have been wounded.

Bang! Enemy fighters open fire on you from a nearby ridge. You drop to the ground behind some rocks. You return fire with your M4 rifle.

Turn the page.

A soldier tracks the enemy through the scope of his sniper rifle.

But the enemy is also taking cover, and you can't get a clean shot. Your back is to the slope. There's a rise about 5 feet up. If you climb it, you might have a better shooting angle. But you'd also be making yourself a target.

To stay where you are, go to page **29**.

To climb up for a better shooting angle, turn to page **36**.

You've got cover here. There's no reason to put yourself at risk. You're sure that someone has already called in an airstrike on the enemy's position. Sure enough, after a 20-minute firefight, you hear the roar of F-15 fighter jets overhead. The jets drop several bombs on the enemy. You feel the shock waves from the explosions as the bombs fall. The enemy has no chance against their force.

You've won the battle, but yet another Ranger was killed in the final fight. A rescue team arrives after sunset. It was a costly battle. Seven American lives were lost, including three Rangers. You will miss the friends you lost, and you know that the war is just beginning for you.

29

## THE END

To follow another path, turn to page 11.
To read the conclusion, turn to page 103.

Your fellow Rangers scramble for cover, but you can't leave Doss behind. You dive down beside him. He's unconscious, and you don't have any way to stop the bleeding. You dash toward the helicopter, hoping you'll find first aid equipment there.

Just then the enemy fires another RPG though the cockpit. The weapon strikes an oxygen tank, which explodes in a ball of fire. You have no chance of surviving the blast. But at least you die a hero.

## THE END

To follow another path, turn to page 11.
To read the conclusion, turn to page 103.

"Our men are in trouble. Get us down there!"
you shout. Harbo reacts immediately, swinging
the Chinook around and descending. "Fire at
will," you tell your gunners.

The sound of two miniguns rattles through
the helicopter. But you know that the gunners are
firing blind. The enemy forces are well hidden.

The enemy returns fire. You can hear bullets
clanging off the Chinook's main body. "We'll all
be killed if we stay here!" shouts Harbo.

He's right. You're about to order a retreat
when a rocket-propelled grenade hits the
Chinook. The helicopter lurches and then falls.
The last thing you see is the rapidly approaching
mountainside.

## THE END

To follow another path, turn to page 11.
To read the conclusion, turn to page 103.

As a mortar blast sends a plume of snow into the air, you decide that this climb is too dangerous. How can your men possibly climb a mountain while under fire from the enemy? Maybe if you regroup at the helicopter, you can find a better way to help the Mustang 1 team.

"Fall back," you order your men. "Return to the landing zone. We have to find another way."

The way down is easier. But as you lead your men down the slope, you begin to question your decision. Have you just doomed the Mustang 1 team to save your own team? Will any help be able to reach them in time?

By the time you speak to your commanding officer, you know that your military career is over. You disobeyed an order and abandoned the soldiers who desperately needed your help. Without your support, they never had a chance. You will have to live with that for the rest of your life.

## THE END

To follow another path, turn to page 11.
To read the conclusion, turn to page 103.

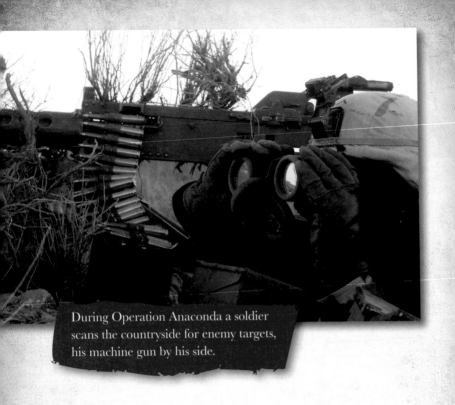

During Operation Anaconda a soldier scans the countryside for enemy targets, his machine gun by his side.

34     "If we hit the enemy now, they won't be prepared," you tell Captain Reynolds. "Every minute we waste is a minute they have to prepare."

You can see that Reynolds doesn't like the idea. But he doesn't have many options. He agrees. It's a desperate attempt, but you are among the best soldiers in the world. If anyone can do it, you can.

You charge the enemy bunker, rushing up the rocky slope. You're met immediately by enemy fire. You hear one man fall, then another. You return fire, but it's hopeless. You just don't have the numbers. An enemy shot hits you in the shoulder and spins you around. You slam onto the slope, smashing your head on a rock.

Unconscious, you never feel the rest of the bullets hit your body. You become another casualty of the battle.

## THE END

To follow another path, turn to page 11.
To read the conclusion, turn to page 103.

Just a few feet up, and you'd have a much better shot at your enemy. You carefully creep up the slope, trying not to draw attention to yourself. You were right. From here you have a line of sight toward one of the enemy positions. You raise your rifle and ... pop!

Your chest erupts with pain. You fall to the ground and lie there as blood seeps from your wound. After what seems like forever, you hear the roar of jets and the explosions of bombs being dropped on the enemy. Your men have won, but you won't be alive to share in the victory.

## THE END

To follow another path, turn to page 11.
To read the conclusion, turn to page 103.

U.S. soldiers search for Taliban insurgents believed to be hiding in caves.

An Army medic prepares to leave Bagram Airfield as part of Task Force Muleskinner.

# CHAPTER 3

# Task Force Muleskinner

You are a sergeant with the 1086th Transportation Company—better known as Task Force Muleskinner. Your convoy is just south of the city of Kabul, rumbling along the dusty Kabul–Kandahar Highway. This two-lane road cuts through eastern Afghanistan. You and the rest of your unit call it A1. You admire the mountains on either side of you. The scenery is very different from the swamps and cypress forests of Louisiana, your National Guard unit's home state.

39

Turn the page.

As the sun pokes over the mountains to your east, it spreads across the valley's floor. You are about 15 hours into what was supposed to be a 20-hour, nonstop trek from Bagram Airfield to Forward Operating Base (FOB) Warrior. You were delayed a few hours back in Kabul when one of the trucks in your convoy broke down.

Specialist Stephanie Miller sits beside you in the driver's seat of the lead truck. You bounce along in a large Mine Resistant Ambush Protected (MRAP) vehicle. You need to keep a slow and steady pace because of the mine roller attached to the front of the MRAP. Should there be an improvised explosive device (IED) in your path, the miner roller will hit the mine before your vehicle does. It will take the brunt of the blast and leave your MRAP unharmed.

An Operation Muleskinner convoy makes its way through the dusty streets of Kabul.

A1 is known as one of the country's deadliest highways. Your gunner, Specialist Brian Lee, rides up in the MRAP's gun turret. He rests one arm on an M240B machine gun as he scans the road ahead.

Turn the page.

Jingle trucks are common sights on the highways of Afghanistan.

You glance back. Five MRAPs trail you. They are mixed in with more than a dozen jingle trucks. These freight trucks add a splash of color to the desert landscape. They are painted with bright colors and designs. Wind chimes and chains dangle from their front bumpers, which is how they earned their nickname. The U.S. military hired the Afghan drivers of these trucks to haul food, fuel, and other supplies.

The convoy approaches the intersection with the Tangi Road. U.S. soldiers call this narrow stretch of highway Route Georgia. It heads east through the mountains. Just after the intersection, you see a small, overturned truck blocking your path.

To move the truck off the road and keep heading down the highway, turn to page **44.**

To turn onto Route Georgia and avoid the blocked road, turn to page **46.**

As you approach the overturned truck on A1, you radio your base back at the airfield. You tell them about the truck in your path.

Captain James Lott's voice crackles back at you, "You're already 5 hours behind schedule. Don't let this delay you much longer."

A soldier prepares the gunner's nest of her MRAP with its attached mine roller.

"Yes, sir," you snap.

"Stay safe, Sergeant," Lott says before signing off.

Then you signal to Sergeant Jonathan White in the MRAP directly behind you. His vehicle doesn't have a mine roller attached, so it can travel faster than yours. White speeds ahead to check out the situation.

To have White push the truck out of the way, turn to page **49.**

To have White stop to check for IEDs first, turn to page **59.**

You radio your base back at the airfield. "There's a truck overturned on A1, and it could be an ambush. Permission requested to turn off onto Route Georgia."

Captain James Lott's voice crackles over the radio. "That's the scenic route, Sergeant, but we've had an increase in attacks along A1 this week. Permission granted."

"Yes, sir," you reply.

The convoy follows your lead and turns onto Route Georgia. The trucks rumble down the winding highway. A few hours later you turn south onto the Kabul-Gardez Highway, and eventually you turn west onto the Ghazni-Gardez Road. Plans are in the works to develop it into a major highway next year, in 2011. But now it's just a rough dirt road, which will lead you back to A1 and your final destination.

Every so often, Lee raps on the roof of the MRAP when he sees debris by the side of the road or a pile of rocks. Both are telltale signs of IEDs. But thankfully what he has spotted so far has been just garbage and mounds of gravel.

A U.S. soldier mans an automatic weapon near the back of a convoy.

Turn the page.

You're about an hour from Ghazni when you take your eyes off the road for a few seconds. Boom! You've hit an IED!

Luckily you have the mine roller attached to the front of your MRAP. The explosion throws the mine roller into the air and rocks your MRAP back, creating a cloud of debris. You, Miller, and Lee are shaken but unharmed.

48

To stop and check for damage, turn to page **55.**

To keep moving, turn to page **62.**

As Sergeant White's MRAP races ahead of you, Miller taps the brakes on your vehicle. The rest of the convoy slows with you.

"Don't bring us to a complete stop if you don't have to," you tell her. "We want to keep rolling in case this is an ambush."

"Sure thing, Sergeant," she replies.

The overturned truck lurches as the bumper of White's MRAP grinds against it. The truck moves forward, screeching as steel grates against pavement.

Boom! White's MRAP is covered in a cloud of debris and dust. Then you hear the ping of bullets as they hit your MRAP's armored plating.

Turn the page.

It's an ambush! Lee returns fire. The other MRAPs spread out on either side of the convoy.

Out in the desert, Taliban insurgents hide behind distant berms of sand. They fire at your convoy from the cover of dips in the terrain. Your gunners return fire.

To keep moving, go to page **51**.

To stay and fight, turn to page **64**.

"White, what's your status?" you shout over the radio.

You hold your breath as seconds pass.

"Shaken and stirred," White replies. "But we're still rolling. Road is clear. I repeat. Road is clear."

This is exactly what the MRAPs were built for—to protect soldiers from IED blasts.

"Go, go, go!" you bark over the radio to the rest of the convoy. The jingle truck engines rev, and the trucks lumber forward. You speed through the cloud of debris into daylight. Lee continues to fire at the insurgents. Up ahead, you see White's MRAP limping along. Once you're away from this ambush, you can stop to make any needed repairs. For now, though, you need to keep going.

51

Turn the page.

A soldier with Task Force Muleskinner feeds rounds of ammunition into the gunner's nest of an MRAP.

Boom! The ground along the side of the road explodes, showering a jingle truck with dirt and rock. The insurgents are attacking with rocket-propelled grenades (RPGs). But with your gunners firing back, they don't have time to take accurate aim. A few more RPGs explode, but they hit off target.

All the trucks get through safely, including the rest of your MRAPs. Once clear of the ambush, you look back. Lee is slumped in the rear of the vehicle.

"I took a piece of shrapnel," he says. Blood seeps between his fingers as he tries to stop the flow.

When you are safely away from the ambush site, you stop to have Lee's wound dressed. You order him back into one of the supporting MRAPs. Specialist Keenan Matthews takes his place in the gun turret. Meanwhile, a mechanic checks out White's MRAP. It survived the IED blast with nothing more than a few dents.

53

Turn the page.

The final leg of your trip takes you over winding, mountainous roads and through war-torn villages. As you drive up a mountain slope, a jingle truck breaks down. Steam hisses from under its hood. Asif Qadir, the truck's owner, shrugs his shoulders in frustration when you ask if he can get it running again.

To leave the truck, turn to page **58**.
To repair the truck, turn to page **67**.

You signal to the rest of the convoy. It screeches to a halt. The MRAPs spread out on either side of the jingle trucks. The gunners scan the horizon with their M240Bs ready.

When the dust settles, you see that the mine roller was blown off and is upside down. All eight of its wheels are scattered around it. You call one of the jingle trucks forward. On its flatbed is another mine roller. Several soldiers push the twisted heap of the old roller to the side of the road. They attach the new roller to the MRAP.

Once you get back into your MRAP, you notice Lee slumped in the rear of your vehicle. Miller is attending to his wound.

"He took a piece of shrapnel," she says.

Turn the page.

You order Lee back into one of the supporting MRAPs. Specialist Keenan Matthews takes his place in the gun turret. Then you are rolling again.

You've only gone about 100 yards when Matthews raps on the hood. He has spotted something suspicious alongside the road. It's a fresh pile of debris. You call a halt to check for IEDs.

Sure enough, there is a tangle of wires and explosives tucked under the pile of rubble. The MRAPs behind you spread out. Their gunners scan the horizon for danger as you have the IED disarmed.

You're quickly back on your way. You reconnect with A1 near Ghazni. Everything is going smoothly until one of the jingle trucks suddenly stops. The engine appears to have overheated. Asif Qadir, the truck's owner, tells you he's not sure if he can fix it.

To leave the truck, turn to page **58**.
To repair the truck, turn to page **67**.

Your convoy is running late. It has been attacked. You have a wounded soldier, and you don't want to take any further risks. Qadir doesn't like the idea of leaving his truck behind, but you order everyone forward.

You radio your base back at the airfield to notify them of the disabled truck. You're able to transfer its contents to other trucks.

"Mount up, people!" you shout once the supplies have been moved. "We need to keep rolling. We're already behind schedule."

58

You're grateful that the final section of your trip is uneventful. As you drive through FOB Warrior's gates, you let out a sigh of relief. Despite the problems, you can count your mission a success.

## THE END

To follow another path, turn to page 11.
To read the conclusion, turn to page 103.

IED blasts destroy roads and make travel difficult in Afghanistan.

Sergeant White's MRAP stops next to the overturned truck. The rest of the convoy grinds to a halt behind him.

Specialist Rachel Morales gets out of White's MRAP. Minesweeper in hand, she slowly walks forward, checking the area in front of her. As she starts around the side of the overturned truck, Morales signals that she has found an explosive.

Turn the page.

Suddenly you hear the ping of bullets striking the armored plating of your vehicle. In front of you, Morales takes cover behind the overturned truck.

"It's an ambush!" you shout over the radio. "Defensive positions!"

The MRAPs behind you spread out on either side of the convoy. Their gunners rattle off several rounds.

In the distance Taliban insurgents hide behind sandy berms. They use the uneven desert terrain for cover as they fire at your convoy.

You have no choice but to hold your ground. The jingle trucks won't be able to get around the overturned truck, which is wired with explosives. They are also too cumbersome to turn around in the middle of a firefight.

Boom! A jingle truck carrying fuel explodes into flames. The heat washes over you. The insurgents are firing RPGs at you. There is another boom as another jingle truck is hit. And another! Two more trucks explode into balls of fire.

Just as suddenly as they appeared, the enemy fighters vanish into the desert. Their ambush was a success. Five trucks were hit.

You radio into base to report the incident. With nearly a third of the supply trucks lost, this mission is a failure. Three soldiers under your command were injured during the firefight. You blame yourself for their wounds, but you're thankful no one was killed.

61

## THE END

To follow another path, turn to page 11.
To read the conclusion, turn to page 103.

The mine roller is a mangled mess in front of your MRAP, but you know you can't stop. This could be an ambush.

"Keep going!" you bark over the radio. The rest of the convoy follows your lead.

A few hundred feet down the road, another blast lifts your vehicle off the ground and throws it on its side.

You are slammed hard against the passenger door. Everything goes black.

When you come to, a medic is treating a wound on your forehead. Your arm hangs limp at your side.

Sergeant White leans over you.

"Both Miller and Lee will be OK," he says. "But your MRAP is scrap metal."

A soldier adjusts a machine gun on her MRAP during Operation Muleskinner.

The MRAP did its job and protected you from a deadly injury, but you will be laid up for weeks with a broken arm. You're grateful it wasn't worse.

63

## THE END

To follow another path, turn to page 11.
To read the conclusion, turn to page 103.

You radio to White, "What's your status? Is the road clear?"

"We're limping along," White responds. "But it's clear."

"Keep the convoy moving," you order. "We'll cover you."

You think the best way to defend the convoy is to draw the insurgents' fire away from the jingle trucks. You order your unit to engage the enemy.

The MRAPs fire on the enemy. The insurgents take cover as machine gun rounds thud into the sand around them. Their AK-47s and old rifles are no match for your weapons. Slowly your forces inch forward, away from the convoy and toward the insurgents. They begin to retreat.

Behind you, the convoy keeps moving forward. In a few minutes, all the trucks will be safely past the overturned truck.

Boom! The ground explodes in front of an MRAP. To your right and along a distant ridge, another group of insurgents attacks with RPGs.

You order Lee to direct his fire at them. His M240B may be powerful, but it isn't very accurate. The insurgents are able to take aim as bullets whiz by them.

Boom! The roar of the blast deafens you. Your MRAP is rocked back. Miller goes limp in her seat. You try to reach over to see if she's OK, but your arm won't respond. It's broken.

65

"Lee, are you OK?" you shout to your gunner.

There's no response.

Turn the page.

As you look out the shattered glass of your passenger window, you realize your mistake. Your unit isn't a fighting force, and you are too few in number. All the other MRAPs are under heavy fire. There is no one to come to your aid.

Slowly your world goes black as pain overwhelms you.

**THE END**

To follow another path, turn to page 11.
To read the conclusion, turn to page 103.

A soldier loads supplies into an MRAP, part of a convoy headed to FOB Warrior.

You call the convoy to a halt. Even though you are already behind schedule, you don't want to lose any supplies.

Turn the page.

The MRAPs spread out protectively around the convoy. Their gunners scan the mountains surrounding you for any danger.

After nearly an hour, you go over to the stalled truck. Two Afghans and one of your soldiers are at the front of the truck with their arms elbow deep in the engine.

"How much longer?" you ask the soldier. He just shakes his head.

Maybe this was a mistake. You are already running late. You are about to reconsider your decision when a shot rings out, echoing off the distant mountains.

You land face down in the dirt, unsure of what happened. The last thing you hear is the rattling of machine gun fire and someone screaming for a medic.

## THE END

To follow another path, turn to page 11.
To read the conclusion, turn to page 103.

A Marine with the 1st Battalion aims at the enemy during Operation Moshtarak.

# CHAPTER 4

# Marines in Marjah

You shrug your shoulders. Gear weighs heavily on them. You feel as if you and the soldiers under your command have been standing around for hours. You're a member of the 1st Battalion, 6th Marines. Your squad is at Camp Dwyer awaiting its final orders.

You check your watch. It is 2:15 a.m. on February 13, 2010. Somewhere in the darkness, U.S. Special Forces are sneaking toward the city of Marjah in southern Afghanistan. Their mission is to secure several helicopter landing sites. Once that is done, your part of Operation Moshtarak will be under way.

71

Turn the page.

With the war in Afghanistan dragging on, U.S military commanders want to take the fight to the Taliban. Insurgents are threatening the safety of civilians in Afghanistan's Helmand Province. Operation Moshtarak is designed to take the area from the insurgents. It will also be the first operation led by the Afghan army. Your squad includes a team of soldiers from the Afghan National Army. You hope that with them by your side, you will be able to win the support of the Afghan people.

But first Marjah needs to be freed from Taliban control. Reports say that as many as 1,000 insurgents roam the city. Your goal is to secure a group of buildings within the city.

Marines board helicopters in the dead of night, heading to Marjah.

Just before 4:00 a.m., Captain Ryan Sparks, commanding officer of Bravo Company, walks through the ranks of waiting Marines. He reminds you not to fire unless fired upon. Harming civilians will put your mission at risk. "Now get to your birds, men!" he orders.

Turn the page.

You and the three teams that form your squad, along with the Afghan soldiers, climb into CH-53 Super Stallion helicopters. Their blades whir, drowning out all other sounds. Within minutes you are airborne and speeding through the night.

Before your boots hit the ground, you pull on your night vision goggles. It is still dark, and the first part of the mission will be tricky. You land on the outskirts of Marjah. You need to find cover before daybreak.

To head into town across a field, go to page **75.**
To head into town on the road, turn to page **78.**

You signal your squad to head for the field. In the green glow of your night vision goggles, you see there is a narrow canal to cross. You slosh through its shallow waters and then up its muddy bank. An empty field spreads out before you. About 200 yards past the canal is a building that you could use for cover. And beyond that is the group of two-story buildings that you have been ordered to secure.

Two soldiers with minesweepers take the lead. As quickly as they can, they check the ground for improvised explosive devices. IEDs. are one of the biggest threats to Allied forces.

You and the rest of your squad spread out in two columns behind the sweeping soldiers. With rifles raised, you keep a lookout for snipers.

Turn the page.

One of the sweepers flags an explosive, and then he veers to the right. You don't have time to disarm it now. Once the area is secure, a mine plow will clear the field.

As you wait, the sky turns from black to a deep blue, so you stash your goggles. This is taking longer than you had hoped. Your squad will be easy targets for snipers if you don't reach cover before sunrise.

To keep heading across the field, turn to page **80.**
To go back and take cover in the canal, turn to page **89.**

Wearing night vision goggles, a soldier carefully looks for enemy insurgents.

You signal your squad to head down the road.

Two soldiers with minesweepers take the lead. They check for improvised explosive devices (IEDs) alongside the road. You and the rest of your squad spread out behind them and slowly inch forward.

To your left, the ground drops away. There is a narrow canal running alongside the road. Up ahead is a building you could use for cover. And beyond is the group of buildings that you have been ordered to secure.

The going is slow as the minesweepers do their jobs. While you wait, you watch the sky lighten. You put away your night vision goggles.

Before long it will be daylight, and you could easily be targets for insurgents.

"Keep an eye on the rooftops for snipers," you warn your squad members.

The Marines nod as they scan nearby buildings for danger.

You are about 20 yards from the buildings when the private next to you whispers, "Sniper!" He points off in the distance.

Your squad needs to find cover. And it needs to find it fast, before the sniper takes aim.

To keep heading down the road, turn to page **83.**

To take cover in the canal, turn to page **89.**

The minesweepers are just 20 feet from the building when you hear the familiar crack of a Lee-Enfield, a rifle used by snipers in the area. The ground explodes inches from your right foot.

"Move! Move!" you order your men.

As you dart for cover, you hear another shot. No one is hit.

"Anyone see where the shots came from?" you ask.

Several Marines point around to the other side of the building.

You peek around a corner. A few hundred yards ahead of you is the cluster of buildings that you have been ordered to secure. They could be the source of the sniper fire.

A soldier searches the ground for IEDs in Afghanistan.

You also see two men standing off to the side of the buildings. Each holds something long and thin. They could be carrying sniper rifles. You aren't sure from this distance.

Turn the page.

"What do you see?" someone behind you asks.

"Two men," you say.

"Must be the snipers," another Marine says. "Should we take them out?"

Captain Sparks ordered you not to fire unless you are fired upon. But what if the men are snipers?

To wait to see what they do, turn to page **86.**

To fire on the men, turn to page **92.**

"Move!" you order your men.

The Marines crouch low as they dash forward. You reach the cover of the building without taking any fire. Once there, you quickly scan the nearby rooftops. You don't see the sniper that the Marine pointed out.

But off in the distance, you hear the crack of a Lee-Enfield. Snipers in the area often use these old rifles because they are more accurate than AK-47 automatic rifles.

On the other side of the building you are hiding behind is the group of buildings you need to secure. There is at least 50 yards of open space between them and you. It is daylight, and you have already seen one sniper.

Turn the page.

You don't want to take the time to sweep the area of IEDs until you have a more secure position. You order 1st team to deploy an Anti-Personnel Obstacle Breaching System (APOBS). The APOBS is designed to explode when set off, safely detonating nearby land mines in the process.

Two members of the team set up the APOBS a short distance from the building you're behind. Then you order everyone to take cover.

When the APOBS fires, it shoots a rocket. Behind the rocket trails a line charge, which looks like a fire hose filled with grenades. The grenades explode as they hit the ground, detonating any nearby mines. When you peek around the building, you see the path of broken ground that the APOBS cleared.

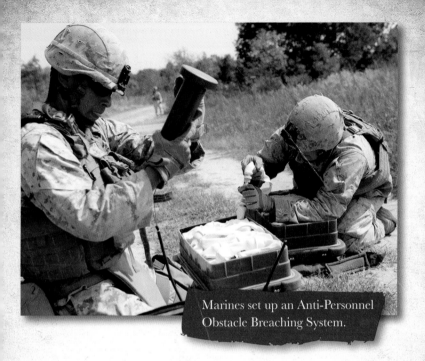

Marines set up an Anti-Personnel
Obstacle Breaching System.

The ground between the buildings is clear,
but you still have to worry about the sniper.
You quickly have to decide what to do.

To rush into the building yourself, turn to page **96.**

To order 2nd team and the Afghan soldiers in,
turn to page **99.**

You send 3rd team around to the right of the building and 2nd team to the left. First team and the Afghan soldiers cover your squad's flank. As the teams spread out, they use dips in the uneven ground for cover.

Then you wait. Several minutes pass before the two men notice you peeking around the corner. One raises his arms in the air. It looks like he is holding a hoe used for farm work. He waves it to get your attention. The other drops what he's holding and motions toward one of the buildings.

You lean out from your hiding spot to look in the direction he's pointing. Then you spot it. On the second floor of one of the buildings is a crack a few feet wide.

From that vantage point, a sniper would have a clear view of the field you just crossed. The two men are warning you of danger.

Just then, you hear a shot. A bullet whizzes inches from your face. You duck for cover. You need to decide on a method of counterattack—right now.

To call for a drone strike, turn to page **88.**
To attack with a rocket, turn to page **94.**

You radio to your base the coordinates of the building with the sniper and request a drone strike.

While you wait for a response, you carefully peek around the corner. You wave for the two men to move away from the group of buildings. They dash for nearby trees.

Several long moments later, the radio crackles to life. "Request denied. Repeat. Request denied."

You hear nearby squad members grumble. There won't be any help from the air today. You have no other choice but to attack.

Turn to page **94.**

You signal your squad to take cover in the canal. The water splashes as your boots sink into the thick mud. Just then, a shot whizzes by you.

"Down! Down!" you yell to your squad members. They duck below the canal's muddy bank.

You didn't see anyone on the rooftops of the surrounding buildings. But insurgents could be hiding inside one of them. From your distant location, they would be nearly impossible to see.

You radio your platoon commander to tell him of the situation.

89

"Can you get a bead on the sniper?" he asks.

Turn the page.

You raise your head to glance over the rim of the bank. Just then, there's a crack of another shot. Searing pain shoots through your left shoulder. "I'm hit," you yell. "Everyone, stay down!"

One of your men immediately radios a medevac helicopter for you. It arrives within two minutes.

The medics strap you on a gurney and load you into the helicopter. Your squad will continue today's mission, but your part is over. You're determined to recover from your wound as soon as possible and lead your squad once again.

Marines carry a wounded comrade to a waiting helicopter.

# THE END

To follow another path, turn to page 11.
To read the conclusion, turn to page 103.

You decide you can't risk your men being shot. You send 3rd team around to the right of the building and 2nd team to the left. First team stays with you while the Afghan soldiers cover your squad's flank. When everyone is in position, you order 1st team to take out the two men. They peek around the corners of the building and aim.

As the soldiers fire, one of the men crumples to the ground. The other drops what he was holding and waves his hands frantically in the air.

Suddenly, the radio crackles. Then you hear your platoon commander's voice, "Corporal, you were ordered not to fire unless fired upon. Was that clear?"

"Yes, sir!" you reply.

"Those were civilians you fired at!"

Your heart sinks as you realize you just ordered an innocent civilian shot. Your actions could jeopardize the mission. Another squad will move in to secure the buildings. Your role in today's mission is over, and you likely face punishment when you get back to base.

**THE END**

To follow another path, turn to page 11.
To read the conclusion, turn to page 103.

You signal to Lance Corporal Henry Suarez in 1st team. He unslings a Shoulder-launched Multipurpose Assault Weapon (SMAW). While Suarez prepares the rocket launcher, you tell him where to fire.

Suarez crouches next to the building. He takes careful aim as he pokes around the corner. Then there's a loud thump as the rocket is launched. Boom!

You risk looking around the corner. The section of building where the sniper was hiding has been blown away. All that is left is crumbling mortar.

With the enemy assumed dead, you order your men forward. They quickly reach the group of buildings without taking any more fire. Then you search the area for IEDs. Once it is cleared, you call your platoon commander to tell him that you have secured the buildings. Your mission is a success.

## THE END

To follow another path, turn to page 11.
To read the conclusion, turn to page 103.

U.S. soldiers fire on the enemy during Operation Moshtarak.

You quickly make your way toward the group of buildings. All the while, you and your men are scanning nearby rooftops for snipers.

You notice a group of people gathered near some homes about 100 yards away. You are not sure what they are doing, but at least they are not firing at you. They could be civilians. But to be safe, you order 3rd team to lag behind and keep an eye on them.

"Don't fire unless they start shooting," you say.

As you reach the buildings, 2nd team spreads out to the right. Third team moves to the left, where its members can keep an eye on the people in the distance. The Afghan soldiers stay behind to cover your flank as you enter the building with 1st team.

You check the door. It's locked.

"Break it down," you order the soldier next to you.

Turn the page.

He steps back and kicks the door. It rattles. Wood splinters and cracks. One more try, and the door gives way. Weapons ready, you rush in.

You realize your mistake when you feel a slight tug on your left foot. You hit a trip wire. A loud boom rocks the building. You and the men around you die as shrapnel whizzes through the air.

**THE END**

To follow another path, turn to page 11.
To read the conclusion, turn to page 103.

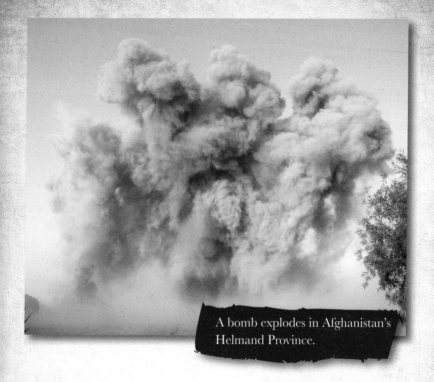

A bomb explodes in Afghanistan's Helmand Province.

You order your men forward. As you head down the path that the APOBS cleared, your men scan nearby rooftops for snipers.

To your left, you notice several people gathered in front of a group of houses. You are not sure if they are civilians, but they are not firing at you. So you keep moving, with 3rd team lagging behind to keep an eye on them.

As you reach the buildings, you order 3rd team to spread out and secure the area. You stay with 1st team as the Afghan soldiers and 2nd team move to enter one of the buildings.

Just then some of the people watching you start to wave frantically. A man shouts something in Pashto, a language spoken in Afghanistan.

The Afghan soldiers and 2nd team Marines freeze and slowly back away from the building's doorway. "What did he say?" you ask them.

"He say bomb, there," one of the Afghan soldiers says in broken English as he points at the door in front of him.

This is exactly why Afghan soldiers are part of your squad—to get the support of the residents.

"Thank him for the warning," you tell the soldier, who then shouts something back at the civilian.

Just inside the door, you find a well-hidden trip wire leading to a large IED. You realize how lucky your squad was. Without the help of the people living here, you may never have spotted the dangerous explosive. After disarming it, you call your platoon commander to tell him that you have secured the buildings. Your mission is a success—thanks in no small part to the Afghan man who helped you.

## THE END

To follow another path, turn to page 11.
To read the conclusion, turn to page 103.

A Chinook helicopter lands in eastern Afghanistan during the successful Operation Anaconda.

# CHAPTER 5

# Success and Failure

The Afghanistan war is a war unlike most conflicts in U.S. history. Troops aren't fighting an established army, as they did in World War I and World War II. The enemy Taliban and al-Qaeda fighters are only loosely organized.

U.S. troops have won many victories during the war. Operation Anaconda was a success, with Allied troops taking control of several key areas of southern Afghanistan. So was Operation Moshtarak. But efforts to finally defeat insurgent forces have failed. Afghanistan's democratic government remains very much at risk of violence and overthrow.

103

Turn the page.

Some people question how the United States and its allies can ever hope to truly win the war. They've captured or killed many al-Qaeda and Taliban leaders, but new ones step in to take their places. Many people viewed the death of Osama bin Laden as a major victory. But in truth, bin Laden's role in the war at the time was minimal. His death was more a matter of justice than it was of military strategy.

Afghanistan's future remains very much in question. Can Allied troops ever establish a true peace? Can the Afghan government grow to a level of strength that allows it to police and defend its own nation? Or will the nation fall back into the hands of extremists and terrorists once the Allied troops are gone? There are no easy answers.

U.S. soldiers watch for enemy movement during the long war in Afghanistan.

# TIMELINE

**2001**

**September 11**—Members of the terrorist group al-Qaeda highjack airplanes and fly them into targets in New York City and Washington, D.C.

**September 18**—U.S. President George W. Bush authorizes the use of military force against Afghanistan's Taliban government.

**October 7**—U.S. military begins bombing Taliban forces as part of Operation Enduring Freedom.

**December 7**—Taliban stronghold of Kandahar falls.

**2002**

**March 1**—Operation Anaconda is launched. U.S. and Allied forces drive Taliban fighters from the Shahi-Kot Valley and Arma Mountains.

**2003**—In August the North Atlantic Treaty Organization takes over control of the peacekeeping mission in Kabul.

**2004**—In October Hamid Karzai becomes Afghanistan's first elected president.

**2005**—U.S. troops launch Operation Red Wings in June to drive the enemy out of Kunar Province. It fails, and 19 U.S. soldiers are killed.

**2006**—In May NATO and Afghan troops launch Operation Mountain Thrust in southern Afghanistan. The mission fails.

**2007**—In May U.S., NATO, and Afghan forces kill Taliban commander Mullah Dadullah.

**2008**—Taliban and al-Qaeda forces increase attacks on the Afghan government and on Allied troops.

**2009**

**February 17**—U.S. President Barack Obama orders a troop surge, adding about 17,000 U.S. troops to the war in Afghanistan.

**December 1**—President Obama authorizes sending 30,000 more U.S. soldiers to Afghanistan.

**2010**—In February about 4,500 NATO troops with about 1,000 Afghans launch Operation Moshtarak in Helmand Province. It is a success.

**2011**

**May 1**—U.S. Navy SEALs locate and kill Osama bin Laden in Pakistan.

**June 22**—President Obama announces plans to withdraw 10,000 U.S. troops by year's end.

**2012**—In May members of a group affiliated with the Taliban kill Maulavi Arsala Rahmani, a key member of Afghanistan's High Peace Council.

**2013**—In June NATO gives full control of Afghan security to the Afghan military.

# OTHER PATHS TO EXPLORE

In this book you've explored key moments in the Afghanistan war through the viewpoint of U.S. soldiers and Marines.

Perspectives on history are as varied as the people who lived it. Seeing history from many points of view is an important part of understanding it. Here are ideas for other points of view to explore.

Many Afghan troops have fought alongside U.S. and NATO troops. What would it be like fighting against people from your own country? (Common Core: Key Ideas and Details)

Boys are recruited by al-Qaeda and other organizations to fight against the new Afghan government. Imagine that you were taken at a young age, taught to fight, and told to attack your own country's government. How would you feel about it? (Common Core: Integration of Knowledge and Ideas)

The war isn't just difficult for U.S. troops. It's also tough on their families. What if you had a parent or sibling serving in Afghanistan? Would you feel proud, afraid, or both? (Common Core: Key Ideas and Details)

# READ MORE

**Burgan, Michael.** *Afghanistan*. Vero Beach, Fla.: Rourke Pub., 2009.

**Carlisle, Rodney P.** *Afghanistan War*. New York: Chelsea House, 2010.

**Crawford, Steve.** *War on Terror*. Redding, Conn.: Brown Bear Books, 2010.

**Hunter, Nick.** *Hoping for Peace in Afghanistan*. New York: Gareth Stevens Pub., 2012.

# INTERNET SITES

Use FactHound to find Internet sites related to this book. All of the sites on FactHound have been researched by our staff.

Here's all you do:

Visit *www.facthound.com*

Type in this code: 9781476541907

# GLOSSARY

**ambush** (AM-bush)—a surprise attack

**civilian** (SI-vil-yuhn)—a person not in the military

**convoy** (KAHN-voi)—a group of vehicles that travel together for safety

**flank** (FLANGK)—the far left or right side of a group of soldiers

**improvised explosive device** (IM-pruh-vized ik-SPLOH-siv di-VISSE)—a homemade explosive, known as an IED

**insurgent** (in-SUR-juhnt)—a person who fights against his or her country's government

**mine** (MINE)—a small device that explodes on contact or when an object comes nearby

**shrapnel** (SHRAP-nuhl)—pieces broken off from an explosive device

**sniper** (SNYE-pur)—a soldier trained to shoot at long-distance targets from a hidden place

**squad** (SKWAHD)—a small group of soldiers under a single officer

**Taliban** (TAH-luh-bahn)—a fundamentalist Muslim group that controlled Afghanistan

# BIBLIOGRAPHY

**Graham, Bradley.** "A Wintery Ordeal at 10,000 Feet." *Washington Post.* 25 May 2002. 7 Oct. 2013. http://www. washingtonpost.com/wp-dyn/content/article/2006/10/11/ AR2006101101434.html.

**Marines: Operation Moshtarak.** 7 Oct. 2013. http://www. marines.com/global-impact/toward-chaos/moshtarak

**Naylor, Sean.** *Not a Good Day to Die: The Untold Story of Operation Anaconda.* New York: Berkley Books, 2005.

**"Obama's War."** *Frontline.* PBS. 13 Oct. 2009.

**Purpura, Paul.** "In Afghanistan, Louisiana troops brave roadside bombs while escorting convoys." *Times-Picayune.* 30 May 2012. 7 Oct. 2013. http://www.nola.com/military/index. ssf/2012/05/in_afghanistan_louisiana_troop.html

**Rayment, Sean, Patrick Sawer, and Ben Farmer.** "Afghanistan: First stage of Operation Moshtarek declared a success." *The Telegraph.* 13 Feb. 2010. 7 Oct. 2013. http://www.telegraph.co.uk/news/worldnews/asia/ afghanistan/7230940/Afghanistan-first-stage-of-operation-Moshtarak-declared-a-success.html

**Scar, Sgt. Ken.** "Night Drivers." *National Guard Magazine.* July 2012. 7 Oct. 2013. http://www.nationalguardmagazine. com/publication/?i=118311&p=38

# INDEX